THE SELBY AND DRIFFIELD RAILWAY

By
C. T. Goode

ISBN 1 870313 13 5
72 Woodland Drive, Anlaby, Hull. HU10 7HX

Produced by
Burstwick Print & Publicity Services,
13a Anlaby Rd. Hull HU1 2PJ

Foreword

Completion of this work has been a change and a contrast to the hills and dales of the last one on 'Huddersfield'. Here was a line which virtually slept during the week, a synecure for staff at places such as Bubwith where nothing much happened during the week to disturb the rural peace. In some cases, adjacent stations would be under the eye of one station master who would roll up to keep things ticking over and pay the wages on a Thursday. Unfortunately, I have never found details of this sort of combination, though it is more than likely that Cliffe Common and Hemingbrough would be teamed, as would Bubwith and Highfield. At summer weekends of course it was all action for the signalmen and gate keepers with the passage of holiday traffic, none of which had the slightest effect on the takings of places such as Everingham or Enthorpe.

Mr. Len Bedale was a relief station master towards the end of his career, and relates the following in his own book:

'A rather unusual incident occurred on the parcels side during one of my sessions at Market Weighton. Passenger parcels traffic for stations on the Derwent Valley Light Railway was held at Market Weighton station daily until the departure of the Selby pick-up goods. By a long standing arrangement the traffic was loaded into the tranship wagon, or guard's van of the train on arrival at the platform. On this particular morning there was quite a large quantity of parcels, ranging from mattresses, boxes of cake and tins of paint to day-old chicks. Owing to the cold weather the consignment of chicks had been placed in the porters' room for warmth and shelter. At noon I heard the pick-up goods stop and restart after the parcels had been loaded. Two minutes after this Ivan, the porter, entered my room in a state of dismay. He had overlooked the unfortunate boxes of chicks and they had thus all been left behind.

With some presence of mind I rang up the Porter-signalman at Everingham and told him to hold the goods train there. This done, I went into the station cafe and Taxi service premises. After explaining matters briefly, I tentatively asked the Proprietor if he would be kind enough to take the chicks out to Everingham station in his taxi. He said that he certainly would if possible, but his cafe was full of lunchtime customers. I offered to assist in his absence and my offer was accepted. He threw off his apron, the chicks were loaded on board and off he went to Everingham. I did what I could in the cafe and within thirty minutes he had returned and I think that, secretly, he had enjoyed his mission. He was pleased to inform me that the goods train was waiting and the chicks were now on their way. Then I thanked him for his help in the matter, he refused to accept a penny piece for his services.'

My thanks go the library staff of the National Railway Museum in York and also at Hull and in the Record Office at Beverley. Thanks, too, to Mike Thompson who helped with the photographic selection. There were, as expected, a host taken of excursions on Enthorpe bank, probably the best spotting location during the season for miles around; there are enough prints left to make up a 'scissors and paste 'album!

C. Tony Goode

Anlaby, Hull. 1993

Abbreviations.

DVLR	Derwent Valley Light Railway
H & BR	Hull and Barnsley Railway
H & SR	Hull and Selby Railway
LNER	London and North Eastern Railway
LNWR	London and North Western Railway
L & YR	Lancashire and Yorkshire Railway
L & SR	Leeds and Selby Railway
NER	North Eastern Railway
NMR	North Midland Railway
SB & WRJc.R	Scarborough, Bridlington and West Riding Junction Railway
SX	Not Saturdays
SO	Saturdays Only.

CONTENTS

Transport pre-Hudson ....p. 7
The Railway King ....p. 8
The pattern of railways is begun p.10
Early plans to reach Market Weighton p.11
Cut-backs and completion p.13
Selby and its bridges p.16
Barlby North out to Cliffe Common p.18
Menthorpe Gate to Highfield p.21
Foggathorpe to Everingham p.24
Market Weighton p.27
The climb to Enthorpe p.28
Bainton and Southburn p.30
Down to Driffield p.31
Passenger Services p.34
Experiments in LNER days p.42
Wartime and latterly p.45
The Derwent Valley Light Railway p.49
Appendices P.53

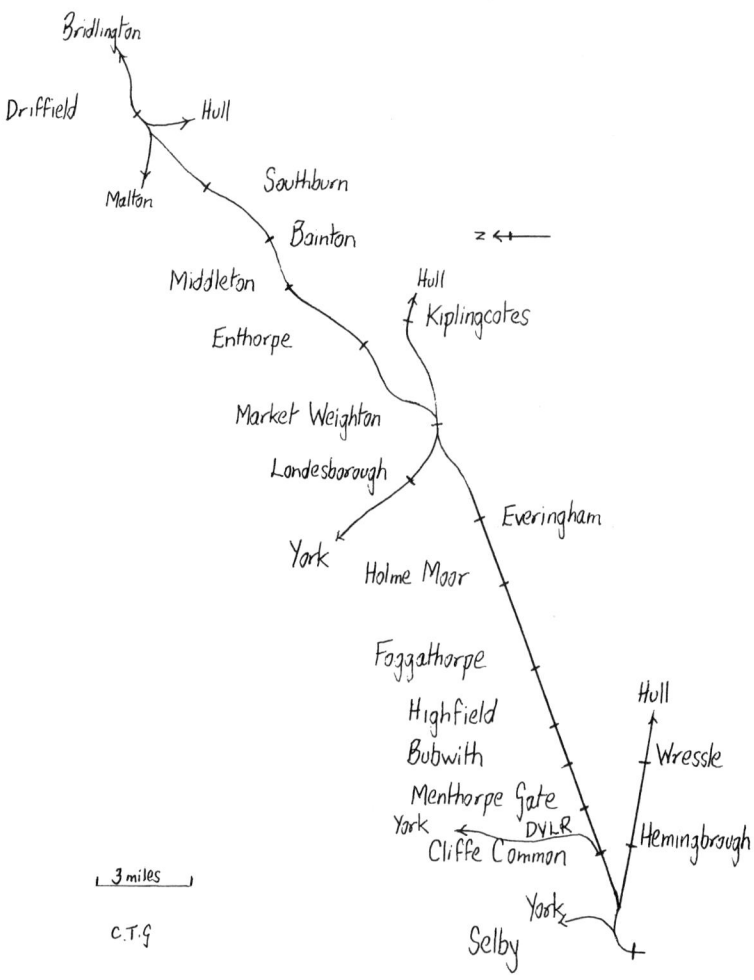

TRANSPORT PRE-HUDSON

The coming of the railways was generally regarded as a blessing to all, not least among the good folk of East Yorkshire who, firstly, could now move freely in and out of the district on business or pleasure, while farmers were now able to market their produce and obtain supplies whenever they were required. The Humber and the river Ouse had of course existed as an artery linking York, Selby and Hull, with the Derwent flowing in from Stamford Bridge and the Pocklington canal running, in turn, into the latter river. From Market Weighton another canal ran southwards to the Humber, while a branch known as Sir Edward Vavasour's canal came into it from Holme-on-Spalding Moor. Into the network of rivers, traffic was fed from the Trent, Aire and Calder rivers, all offering a reliable run of barges and passenger boats, or packets, as they were known; however, all of these were very slow.

The contemporary Earl Fitzwilliam owned most of the local navigation rights in East Yorkshire, especially over the Derwent which passed much grain and animal foodstuffs from mills at Malton and Stamford Bridge. However, being something of an entrepreneur, the Earl took up with the new form of transport as it flourished, and in 1855 sold the Derwent Navigation to the NER for £40,000 at a time when its tonnage conveyed was about the same yearly figure. Use of the river persisted until 1905, under the NER umbrella, though this had fallen to 6,076 tons. The end soon came and weeds and silt took over.

The Market Weighton canal had opened in 1778 and was an important factor in draining the land at the Humber end, as well as transporting local goods. There was a brisk traffic in bricks and tiles from the Broomfleet area. The railway stepped in quickly and bought the canal for a substantial sum, claiming all profits due from navigation. Along with this went the Vavasour branch. The waterway proved to be a money-spinner, gaining many thousands in profit, especially between 1860 and 1872. After this, due to the opening of the railway from Market Weighton to Beverley, the NER allowed things to slide and by 1888 much dredging needed to be done; it became difficult to move tiles from Henry Williamson's works to Market Weighton, and the untroubled waters began to prove to be a hazard to health. In 1900 an Act was secured which closed the Market Weighton canal, apart from a section at the Broomfleet end where activity continued until 1958. The Pocklington canal was navigated until 1932 and thereafter for occasional pleasure craft.

THE RAILWAY KING

The canals mentioned above might be considered to be pre-Hudson, while the new railways in Yorkshire were all-Hudson, for George Hudson was the Railway King. He had no interest in railways as a technical feature, but saw them only as a means of making money, which he managed in plenty, often employing means which were somewhat on the shady side. George was born at Howsham, not far from York, of a farming family and began working as a draper's assistant in that city. On coming into an inheritance of £30,000, a not inconsiderable sum in those days, he prospered and soon became Chairman of the York Banking Company, becoming thrice Lord Mayor. Hudson owned land at Huntington, Shipton, Londesborough and Market Weighton, names which evoke the stations through which his lines were to run. He was eventually accused of overpricing the value of his land when selling plots to the railway, and its recovery brought him shame and bankruptcy. These court appearances resulted in ignominy and rejection by the good people of York, a stain which endured right up to the anniversary of the city's foundation in 1971, when his undoubted benefits to local industry and to commerce in general were acknowledged.

Enthorpe

It is far more pleasant now to dwell on the latter aspects of an interesting man who gave so much in the way of cheap transport at a time of speculation during the Railway Mania of 1845, when the countryside was criss-crossed by schemes to link the insignificant with the indifferent. First in the field in East Yorks. was the Hull & Selby Railway which was a Hudson-backed local venture of the Mania proper and which took a straight and level course east-west along the Humber bank. It was given Parliamentary approval on 21st.June 1836 and opened with éclat on 1st. July 1840.

George Hudson wished to 'escape' from York and form a new link with London; the very first idea in this direction was broached at a meeting held at the Londesborough Arms in York on 30th. December 1833 to discuss the possibility of a line to Leeds, seemingly a roundabout way of reaching London, but one which would meet up with other Hudson interests; the London & Birimingham Railway would be left at Rugby by the Midland Counties Railway which would run to Leicester and Derby, then meeting the North Midland Railway at the last named place to run up to Normanton and Leeds, All of this did materialise, and the journey to Euston was, surprisingly, not much longer than might be expected.

Opposition was in the offing, however, in the shape of the Grand Northern Railway project which would send a line up the eastern side of the country from London through Cambridge to Peterborough, then by way of Lincoln to York. This idea had nothing to do with George Hudson but was the brainchild of Mr. Cundy, a canal man. Swiftly the York-Leeds route was amended to become the York & North Midland, and the line from York to Church Fenton was completed and opened on 29th. May 1839, with a junction at South Milford to the Leeds & Selby Railway to afford a connection with the Leeds and Hull on either side of it. The L & S had been an early entry to the railway field, opening on 22nd. September 1834 and local in nature. The line from York was actually a short cut in the great scheme for reaching London, and it was completed in June 1840 when the remaining portion to Altofts Jc. on the North Midland was opened and services could now run to Normanton. Clever it was in those days-it could never happen-today for the line from Rotherham to Altofts Jc. to open on the same day as that from York, 30th. June 1840, giving a through passage to the south, thus,a passenger train leaving York at 7.30am would take a half hour break in Derby for lunch and be in Euston at 9.30pm. Soon afterwards York-Leeds trains used a spur line at Methley Jc. to the NMR, a device which bullied the little L & S into entering upon a 31 year agreement for lease with Hudson at a rental of £17,000 per annum,for otherwise it was arranged that they would be starved of traffic through Milford until they conformed. The H & S was a more difficult nut to crack though Hudson tried to bring them under his aegis by putting freight back on to the river to and from Hull on the much slower steam tugs. The H & S were also friendly with the M & LR who had reached Normanton via Wakefield and eventually arrived at Goole with its tremendous potential as a seaport. Relations with the H & S were cordial, even though there was no real connection as yet, and an alliance was made, on paper at any rate, from 1st.January 1844, a move which displeased Hudson. In the end however, the great man had his own way, as there were two prominent Hull businessmen in his camp who were H & S shareholders and who enabled him to secure the little company on favourable terms, so that, on 1st. July 1845 the H & S joined the L & S as part of the Y & NM empire, with Hudson as Chairman of the whole.

THE PATTERN OF RAILWAYS IS BEGUN

The jig-saw now needs to be built up, so to speak, from the base line of the Hull & Selby route on the south side of the area. An Act passed on 5th. June 1844 allowed the construction of a line between York and Scarborough which would complete the north boundary; this was for 42 miles of main line with a $6^{1}/_{2}$ mile branch from Malton to Pickering, with designs on linking up with the much older Whitby & Pickering Railway, a company which was also destined for acquisition in due course. The whole of the line and branch was built in under a year at a cost of six thousand pounds per mile, most of it easy going, apart from some curves in the vicinity of Castle Howard. The lines were opened on 7th. July 1845 and the populace enjoyed five days of free travel.

During this period of Railway Mania some 107 miles of railway routes were applied for in East Yorkshire, not all of which, such as the plan for a line between Beverley and Hornsea, succeeded in materialising. During 1845-6 Acts were obtained for what could be termed the north-south boundary of the triangle of East Yorks. lines, namely the stretch from Hull to Bridlington via Beverley, which was opened on 6th. October 1846 and the complementary section from Seamer on the Scarborough line to Bridlington southwards via Filey, opened to Filey on 5th.October 1846, but leaving an ominous gap which was due to the tricky terrain, necessitating some rather vicious curves near Flamborough and five miles at 1 in 92 up from Bridlington station to Speeton. The result was that the final $13^{1}/_{2}$ miles section did not open until 18th. October 1847. The triangle was now complete and anything further east of Hull, that is, the Withernsea and Hornsea branches, though relatively easy to lay on the levels of Holderness, did not appear until June 1853 and March 1864 respectively.

The centre of this East Yorkshire triangle now merits attention, a somewhat difficult area which is divided into flat land to the west and the hilly Wolds to the east, with Market Weighton roughly in the middle. It was this small and undistinguished little market town which took Hudson's fancy as a place on which to concentrate his new railways, one of many such 'victims' up and down the country at this period, and a criss-cross of lines was planned here, with the first half of a proposed York to Beverley line opening to Market Weighton on 3rd. October 1847 and the half of a proposed Selby to Driffield route reaching there on 1st. August 1848. One other line there was which fits into the puzzle at this stage, the Malton & Driffield Junction Railway whose Act was authorised in June 1846. This was a heavily graded, single track branch through the high Wolds, its steepest climb at 1 in 73 or 64 from Malton up to Wharram and with a mile long tunnel at Burdale. The line was not in use before 19th. May 1852, due to the amount of engineering involved. At Malton the line took its main course across the Scarborough line, reached by a spur, to run into a further extension, opened simultaneously, which took traffic to and from the Great North of England main line at Pilmoor, a handy link between the north and the growing resorts on the east coast.

EARLY PLANS TO REACH MARKET WEIGHTON

Matters were now in abeyance at Market Weighton, with two lines arriving from different directions into what was a terminus for the next 17 years. The branch from York had been constructed by Messes. Jackson & Bean with stations built by Burton & Son to the design of G.T.Andrews, all for a total of £116,029. Trains began to run just three days after the deadline on 30th. September 1847. For the Selby branch the contracts were worth £81,598, but things did not proceed so smoothly, as there were disputes over such matters as the number of sidings, siting of coal depots and size of the goods sheds which deferred the opening until 1st. August 1848. There were complaints that the York line stations were too elaborate, especially Pocklington's with its overall roof, though at Burnby there was no cover of any kind in wet weather.

B16 No. 61471 passes Duffield gate with a holiday working   *J.F. Sedgwick*

The official title of the Act for the Selby-Market Weighton line was the York & North Midland Railway (East Riding) Branches No.11 Railway Act of 1846. This allowed a railway from the Hull & Selby Railway in the Parish of Barlby to join an intended railway from or near the city of York to Beverley in the Township and Parish of Market Weighton. In the same Act was the previously mentioned line from Beverley to Hornsea which was not proceeded with. Some 37 parishes were to be traversed, as well as thirteen crossings of public roads. Whereas the execution of the York line went ahead according to plan, as noted, the Selby line was dogged by pitfalls, such as the Rev. J.D. Jefferson's questioning the siting of Bubwith station, one of the more imposing buildings placed to the south of the village; he preferred the stop to be to the east, 'in the high field'. Apparently he had sold some of his land to the company and lost £160 on the deal, leaving him somewhat miffed. In the event,the NER did provide this facility, giving two stops within a short distance of each other. A Mr. Musgrave of Foggathorpe wanted sidings there (the next station), and presumably he was also the gentleman who had his own depot adjacent to the engine shed at Market Weighton station.

There was trouble over the material to be used for constructing the coal depots-was it to be wood or not ? The goods depots, too, were to be lower than those on the York line. At first there were two 'proper' stations, at Bubwith and Holme, both with quite acceptable buildings. There was, later on, a third building of some distinction at Everingham completed during one of the NER bouts of name changing when the original name, Harswell Gate was changed. Stations were also provided at Cliff Common Gate, Duffield Gate, Menthorpe Gate, Foggathorpe Gate and, as mentioned, Harswell Gate. Neither the latter hamlet, nor Everingham was anywhere near the railway. Duffield Gate did not last long, and 'Gate' was discontinued, apart from at Menthorpe. On the opening of the line, eleven permanent way men were employed, plus three coaching dept. staff, costing a total annual sum of £137.16s. Takings in June 1849 were £2,336, made up of £1,335 goods, £924 passenger, £44 parcels, £30 rents and £3 horse and dog conveyance.

The York-Market Weighton line had 22 level crossings in as many miles, a continual source of destruction to man and livestock. In 1851 one John Nicholson was killed by a train after falling asleep with his horse and cart on the Selby line. Not far away, the owner of Portington Hall near Eastrington would return home regularly at night fast asleep in his horse and trap, the horse taking him faithfully over the Hull & Barnsley level crossing. Here it was decided that gates should be kept closed to the road and opened only on request, the keeper operating a swivelling red board with a lamp to warn trains. Such crossings and keepers still survive (near Wressle) and the boards finally went only about five or six years ago.

At Hagg Lane crossing, near Wressle, a Manchester-Hull dmu service is held up by the old cross-bar signal, still in use in the eighties. In this case it had evidently been rotated by mistake.   *C.T. Goode*

CUT BACKS AND COMPETITION

With the freezing of the ambitions of both the routes at Market Weighton, some retrenchment was considered; the Selby line stayed single until 1889 and the York line was earmarked for singling as early as 1853. Huntington station was closed in August 1850, as the income here was minimal. Some stations on the York line were renamed, such as Burnby to Nunburnholme and Shipton to Londesborough. Hudson's own station at Londesborough Park was closed upon the dispersal of his estates. Such renaming to avoid confusion with similar names elsewhere explains why NER stations often bear the names of villages several miles away. There were irregularities in the accounting at some of the York line stations during 1849, and Mr. J. Lee resigned as Station Master of Pocklington soon after an enquiry there in November. He was replaced by Mr. J. Wright at a salary of £1.1s. per week, no great inducement to honesty, it might be felt. Very soon he, too, was moved to Holme on the Selby line and exchanged posts here with Mr. Dooks. Some of the staff were obviously carrying out the spirit of George Hudson a little too realistically at this time!

There was frequent agitation for the completion of the two lines across the Wolds, and in the case of the Beverley line there were obstacles placed in the way by Lord Hotham of Dalton Holme, the large estate across which the line would pass. The Y & NM were in some financial difficulties and it was urged that they should plead this fact and also indicate that they really considered the line to be of little public use. However, others thought differently and a Mr. Bunton wished to press for authority compelling the company to provide the line. Once the NER was established in 1854 that company found itself under the same pressure to complete the line, and if not this, then why not a line from Market Weighton south to Brough and the Hull & Selby? A group of Hull businessmen were particularly interested in such a proposal, which had been part and parcel of the schemes of the H & SR and surveyed by them. George Hudson, had he remained in power, would have approved the line which had been earlier agreed by the Y & NM at a meeting held on 17th. May 1845, as part of a branch off the York-Beverley line, signifying that the company were hoping to have both routes running to Hull, or an option thereon. On 23rd. March 1847, with Mr. Egginton as President, a Hull meeting pushed for an extension of the York-Market Weighton line to Brough as being 'highly desirable and necessary' for the accommodation of the district through which it would pass, and also yielding an ample financial return. This was all made official in 1856, and favoured by the Mayor. Alderman Bannister. A prospectus appeared under the heading of the Hull & Market Weighton Railway Company, offering £10 shares. Sir William Worsley of Hovingham was the leading shareholder, while there were many distinguished lesser lights from North and South Cave. The line was to be level, something of a feat, and would

B16 No. 61431 heads south through Selby with freight c.1960   *P. Cookson*

cost £50,000 with a potential to link Hull with the north of the country. There were those who were fearful as to what the land would do to their lands, physically scarred and with squabbling navvies at first, followed by the hordes of great unwashed from Hull frolicking in the verdure of South Cave. The line never materialised because the NER favoured the other route to Hull via Beverley; had it been built, it would have followed the same route as the old Roman road through Newbald and reached the Selby line west of Brough.

At long last, in 1860 the NER was persuaded to take some action over its Beverley extension. It was reported that only one landowner had quibbled over a price for his land; a fresh Bill was presented to Parliament and an Act was granted on 30th. June 1862 with work beginning in September. One of the sources of dispute with Lord Hotham was, as so often the case where a line crossed somebody's land, the provision of a station for the owner's use, and it was the location which caused the problem in this instance. The NER favoured a site at Goodmanham, a small village just north east of Market Weighton with historic connections as the place where King Edwin of Northumbria was converted to Christianity, a more commercial proposition than Kiplingcotes, especially as the company would be paying for the installation. The latter was favoured by Lord Hotham; it was a remote place with a couple of farms for company, though not far from his racecourse. Another stipulation was that no trains were to pass over the Hotham estate on Sundays, a rule which was honoured by service trains right up to closure. There were other niggles on the part of various landowners to be overcome, plus the difficult terrain in laying out the line, so that opening did not take place until 1st. May 1865 along a single line and with a second station at Cherry Burton. It is believed that the line was doubled, along with the Selby line, in 1889 when traffic had developed, though records show only a single line as late as 1900.

As stated, the lapse of time before anything further was carried out as regards putting railways across the Wolds east and northwards required fresh Acts of Parliament, and in 1884 a proposal offered by an independent company, constituted as the Scarborough, Bridlington & West Riding Junction Railway projected a route from Seamer (Scarborough) actually passing near but missing Bridlington, through Driffield to Market Weighton and thence to Howden, another magnetic place for odd railway schemes; this one was a duplicate of the original idea for a line from Driffield to Market Weighton and of the Selby-Weighton line as it now actually was. Support for the idea was lukewarm and when the SB & WRJR dropped its Market Weighton-Howden intentions, the NER in 1885 reluctantly offered to operate the remaining portion, now between Driffield and Market Weighton only. This section was nominally independent until the Great War, when the NER finally took things over. The Driffield-Seamer idea was dropped in 1887 and construction was due to begin a year earlier but was delayed due to arguments with the NER over kinds of materials to be used. It needed until April 1888 to decided upon whether to place a level crossing at Bainton instead of a bridge, and to construct a station there. The line was laid to high standards and was well fitted to take the heavy seasonal traffic from the West Riding and Midlands on summer weekends. In contrast to the flat and rather dull line to Selby, here was a steeply graded line at 1 in 95/100 up to the isolated station of Enthorpe (one house visible), placed at the start of Lord Hotham's racecourse and at the point where the chalk cutting ended. On the downhill stretch were Middleton, Bainton and Southburn stations before Driffield was reached.

A grimy B1, piloted by V1 No. 67677 pause at Selby on a Hull-Leeds train
P. Cookson

SELBY AND ITS BRIDGES

Selby is an important market town and meeting place of highways crossing the Ouse river, roughly midway between Doncaster and York and between Leeds to the west and Hull further away to the east, a pattern which was to be repeated when the railways came, with the additional traffic from the Midlands and south west via Gascoigne Wood Jc. and Normanton. Eastwards the traffic went to Hull and the coastal resorts through Market Weighton and Driffield along the lines which form the subject of this book. The volume of traffic between north and south predominated, and east-west workings had to be fitted in neatly along with quite an abundance of shunting across from one side of the layout to the other at the station, behind nifty little tank engines.

The town is old, its origins due to the Ouse, here flowing down to Hull from York, dominated by the Abbey which was once familiar on a locally made brand of sauce, but with no other buildings of great distinction. The old main road crossed the river north-south by a wooden swing bridge which was, until last year, owned by a private toll company, since bought out by the council. The railway bridge is a few yards downstream to the east and was originally opened in February 1840 as a double bascule cast iron structure of two lifting flaps each of 92 tons, 192 ft. long and 24 ft. wide and, perhaps incredibly, manually raised. When the Doncaster-York line was opened through Selby in 1871 the bridge was still in daily use and rattled to the passage of up to 200 trains each day though only 17 vessels by water. Nelson of York constructed a new bridge for £22,343 just alongside the old which was opened in 1891. Here was a swing span of 130 ft. offering a clearance of 60 ft. as against 45 ft. for the older one. The span was not centrally pivoted, having the shorter side of 43 ft. over terra firma and loaded with 92 tons of counterweights. There was a single fixed span of 110 ft. 6 in. as a 'run-up'. The swing span had parallel box girders 2 ft. wide with a passage of 26 ft. between them, while the whole was swung on 24 conical rollers resting on a 15 ft. turntable, powered by a high pressure hydraulic system for which an accumulator was housed in a tower on the north bank. Emergency energy was no longer muscle but steam pumps of 52 " X 6 " stroke. With this bridge, built in the house style of the NER, came the end of river supremacy over rail; movements were controlled by Selby North signal box nearby which could freeze everything by reversal of king lever No. 14.

One of the shunters at Selby, J72 No. 68686 waits as an express heads for Doncaster through the centre road. *C.T. Goode*

The bridge exists today and looks as it always did, except for being much more run-down and with a miserable speed restriction of 10 mph across it and with the operating cabin on top raised by a couple of feet for electrification that never came. After the last war it was opened to river traffic some 6-8 times each day, often for up to half an hour if several ships had to be moved at one session. Before moving away from the bridge, one should mention in passing the destructive flooding of the river which took place here in the Spring of 1947, leaving the Abbey looking like the superstructure of a sinking battleship, as was written at the time. There were four lines through the station, which of course became two to cross the bridge and then immediately resumed as four again. On the up side the Hull line came in by spring points to avoid the impossible use of lever operation, while the down slow diverged from the main line south of the bridge, the separated lines being interlaced, or gauntletted over it before going their parallel ways.

BARLBY NORTH OUT TO CLIFFE COMMON

Further north were the Goods Nos.1 and 2 lines on the up side which fed into the up Hull line, giving a total of six running lines here, which were crossed by a works level crossing manned by Barlby signal box on the down side. The works formed the extensive premises of the British Oil & Cake Mills, chiefly on the down or west side here. About one quarter of a mile further on was Barlby North, originally Barlby Jc. which lay in the fork of the 'Y' junction at the place where the York and Hull lines divided. Here the slow and goods lines came in and here, too, was a rather unusual phenomenon for its day in that a main to main facing crossover took down Hull trains to the wrong line for a very short distance to gain the correct down branch line. This was thought to be most daring, especially on a prime railway route, though the practice is quite common nowadays with the single lead junctions in use. The key crossover at Barlby was No. 23 which could originally only be released when the branch points No. 77 were reversed, to avoid the risk of Hull drivers rushing up to York on the wrong line. However,this locking was actually dispensed with when it was found that, at times, working had to be made to Riccall on the wrong line (for some reason), an even more curious state of affairs.

In the sidings on the east side were a couple of highly original NER slotted junior signals, though not part of the Barlby North brigade. One had two arms of the same height pointing the same way and back to back with each other; the other had a single arm but with back to back spectacles each side of the lamp case. They were possibly unique and would have been worth preserving. The principal running lines had two gantries of signals, the larger straddling the convergence of routes. There were two southbound homes, for Main and to No. 1 Goods, two for eastbound Hull and Market Weighton trains and a small arm to the sugar factory sidings over facing points, then four southbound signals for trains off the Hull line to Hull line continued, Nos.1 and 2 Goods lines and Up Siding. The junction of the Market Weighton line occurred off the Hull lines, just beyond where the York line diverged.

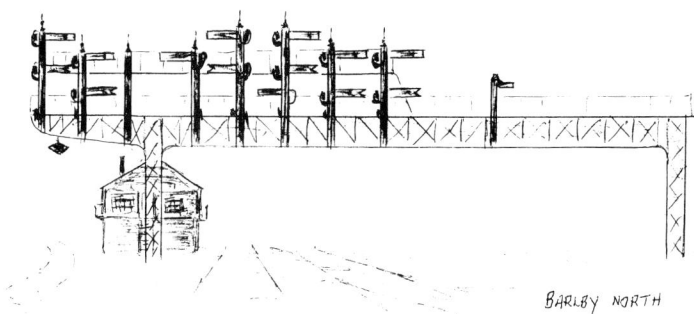

BARLBY NORTH

Barlby North

Barlby North was somewhat unusual as a cabin in that the lever frame was split and placed back to back, with levers 1-55 facing the York side, and 56-95 facing the Hull lines-remember that the box was built within the fork. Activities, though brisk, where not so frequent, as there were in fact 24 spare levers. North of the Hull lines, and following the course of the Market Weighton branch was WD property, a nucleus of small brick sheds obviously arranged for the preparation of explosives and marked 'Powder Magazine' on railway records. A trailing connection led into the down Market Weighton line from here. In the fork of the 'Y' at this junction was a small cabin, Cliffe Jc. which existed along with the then Barlby Jc. certainly in 1908 and which would attend to the Driffield bound services off the Hull lines and manage the WD siding and sugar sidings on the south side. This signal box disappeared after 1923. A king lever, No. 40 in Barlby North box later controlled train staff and ticket working on the single line to Cliffe Common during the 1939-45 war, when the up line was used for the storage of 'crippled' wagons awaiting repair. A wheel chock was placed on the up line to prevent any overrun across the junction. Signals No. 56 and 57, the Outer and Inner Up Homes were set to the right of the line here and were used by up trains when using the down line. Incidentally, the single line arrangement went through to Everingham at this time, as will be seen presently. As the line began life as a single track, and persisted in this form until doubling in 1889, it might be thought that events were following tradition. Originally the exchanging points for staffs were at Cliffe Jc., Highfield for some reason and at Ballast Pit, just short of the west junction at Market Weighton. The first staff was of wood with a single ring round it, the second had two rings, while the last one for the Market Weighton section had three rings. From Cliffe Jc. to Cliffe Common station the straight and level line, which was similar in fact all the way to Market Weighton, set off north eastwards to enter the only cutting on the line and beneath the A63 road, crossing the manned level crossing at Cliffe Common Gate to reach the station at 2m 108 yd., the first layout having a siding to a malthouse on the south side, then the level crossing with the Duffield-Cliffe road with the signal box on the north side,

Cliffe Common signal box C.T. Goode

followed by facing platforms and a three road yard on the south side. There was also a single siding to the roadway on the north side, behind the station building. Where actually was Cliffe, or Cliff, as the place was spelled from time to time? Apart from the Railway Hotel, there is nothing visible on the older maps. However, it lay strung out along the road running south across the Hull & Selby line and meeting the aforementioned A63 road. At the crossing of the latter railway was Cliffe station which, with the fickleness of the NER and with an eye to avoiding confusion to the locals, was changed to Hemingbrough in 1874; this station was closed in 1967 but still lingers by the lineside. Two large maltings were built around 1889, one at Cliffe Common and one at Hemingbrough, and both were used until about 1960. The station layout at Cliffe Common was of course developed round the original single line, as were the others, and with the coming of the Derwent Valley Light Railway in 1912 something bigger was provided which was altered at various times. There was a DVLR platform on the north side to which their trains ran, and a bigger NER signal box resited on the south side. This had 53 levers, of which 21 were spare. There was a facing connection to the DVLR, controlled originally by a branch semaphore, and in 1950 as a ground disc No.22. The 1950 plan gives two facing connections off the

'Black Five' No. 44856 Passes Cliffe Common on a holiday special   J.F. Sedgwick

land, plus both facing and trailing connections to the NER, perhaps optimistically. The author's own notes, taken in April 1948 show a back shunt off the DVLR into the NER sidings. At this time there were still lines of condemned rolling stock on the up line from Market Weighton. The king lever here was No. 20, placed normally for single line working. One reference gives two separate ground frames giving access to the DVLR, one at 336 yd. and the other at 730 yd., though these appear to have vanished in later days. Menthorpe Gate station occurred at 1m. 628 yd. further on after two more level crossings, one of which, South Duffield Gate, was originally a small station serving the little village to the south of the line, 236 souls in 1861. The station was closed in 1884, before the line was doubled.

MENTHORPE GATE TO HIGHFIELD

Menthorpe Gate was a small station with staggered platforms, the down one on the Selby side of the level crossing opposite to the yard of two sidings. The signal box was on the north side, far end of the platform by the crossing, with ten levers, of which two were spare. No.2 was the king lever, to be reversed for single line working on the down line. Beyond the level crossing was, quite simply, the other platform. The road over the crossing was a minor one from Duffield, two miles away and of reasonable size, southwards to the hamlets of Menthorpe and Howthorpe. The population of both remained at a total of about 70 up to 1931.

Menthorpe had a ferry over the Derwent, closed before 1939, while Bowthorpe had its Hall, owned at one time by Sir Robert Walker of Sand Hutton Light Railway fame, up to 1924, after which it changed hands several times and has since become derelict.

B1. No 61087 nears Menthorpe Gate with a working on a summer Saturday
J.F. Sedgwick

On to Bubwith, at 1m. 648 yd., this time with a crossing of the Derwent in company with the road bridge and its many arches close by on the A 163 to the north. Bubwith station had a little more atmosphere than other stations on this line, with a good building on the north side opposite the signal box of eleven levers and adjacent to its modest two road yard with cattle dock. One might suppose that the original single line platform was in front of the building on the north west side of the crossing; the final version came on the east side in the shape of facing platforms. At one time there was a scissors crossover in the main line under the eye of the signalman, possibly to cater for an earlier single line system which would begin here. For the latter single line working, the king lever here was No.8, left normal for single line working on the down line. Bubwith village is a pleasantly wooded, decent sized place half a mile to the north, with a fine 13th. century church next to a meander of the river. At the present time the station enjoys an interesting existence, with the main building in private hands, while the platforms and signal box still survive but in a sort of Sleeping Beauty state, completely choked by wild growth and rapidly maturing saplings. Modern dwellings fill up the gap along the main road between Bubwith and Highfield,1,561 yd. further along the railway. The station was built a little later by the NER, probably as a placebo for local interests, as nothing existed to justify it. There were staggered platforms on each side of the level crossing which was worked by a cabin on the west side and with odd sidings on the up side on each side of the crossing. There was a rather mean single storey building on the down platform and the gatekeeper's house opposite, to the south. Here were 13 levers, and the king lever for single line working on the down line was No.6. One wonders why Highfield was chosen right from the outset as a suitable place to exchange train staffs-possibly it was because the place had less duties and traffic to deal with than elsewhere.

Bubwith station, dereliict befor the undergrowth took over   C.T. Goode

Bubwith station looking east.   D. Thompson

FOGGATHORPE TO EVERINGHAM

Foggathorpe made its mark on the main road in the shape of a public house and a minor crossroads, north to Laytham and south over the railway to a cluster of villages, Gribthorpe, Willitoft and Spaldington. There was Foggathorpe Manor House and the Grange, which probably justified the station, at 1,571 yd. from Highfield, with basic buildings having parallel platforms on the west side of the level crossing and the signal box on the east side, along with what might be termed the standard country station layout of yard to the north, long siding to the south and slip across to the up line in order to gain access to the yard from both directions. There were 13 levers at the signal box, while the king lever here was more than likely No.9, as the author's note is, for once, unclear. The run to the next station at Holme Moor was a longer interval of 2 m. 1,515yd. during which the line crossed the river Foulness and the A163 by a skew level crossing. Holme-upon-Spalding Moor, to give it its full name, is a rather large and sprawling village along the A 163, with yet more to the south by the A 614 road which arrives from the south and joins the first mentioned in the centre, with the grounds of Holme Hall curbed by a long wall on one side. The hall is now a nunnery and was once the home of an ardent Royalist, Sir Marmaduke Langdale. Behind it rises a rather strange hill out of the flatness to about 153 ft., topped by the village church which thus enjoys a fine all-round view. The station building was the second, more substantial one met with so far after Bubwith, to which it was similar, with a two storey portion having its gable end-on to the platform and a bay window overlooking activities thereon, while to one side was a low, single storey attachment with an extension of the roof forward to cover a walkway in front of a couple of rooms for waiting, tickets etc; in short, the house style of the NER hereabouts.

Highfield station, looking east. *D. Thompson*

The premises were on the village (south) side, on the up platform, while the station itself lay some way out of the village to the north west. The small yard lay west of the level crossing on the south side and a siding served a dairy produce factory. The signal box was also on the west down side and had 17 levers, the necessary king lever here for single line working being No.15.

Everingham was the next station at 1 m. 1,688 yd. on a featureless line unrelieved by even a level crossing of any kind. The stop was originally known as Harswell Gate, and the 'Gate' was generally discontinued, except at Menthorpe. Harswell is only a farmstead to the north, with an old manor house, small church and moat, so it was perhaps not surprising that the NER changed to Everingham which lay some three miles to the north, not a large place, but with the 'draw' of the Hall, one of the seats of the Duke of Norfolk, set in pleasant parkland. The railway company were somewhat carried away here and provided the only five ton crane on the branch, in the goods yard. This had three roads on the north side, where was also the station building, another decent one, somewhat different to view, of two storeys with twin gables end-on linked by a transverse section, the recess covered by a canopy at first floor level, quite sumptuous for a remote site. If any aim was intended, it was certainly to impress any visitors to the Norfolk residence. This structure was on the staggered down platform, the up being on the west side of the level crossing. The signal box was opposite the down one, along with a refuge siding. There were 13 levers, and the king lever was No.5, set normally for single line working on the down line.

Holme Moore station, since purchased and spruced up.   *C.T. Goode*

B16 No. 61421 hurries a holiday service through Shipton Lane crossing.
J.F. Sedgwick

Beyond Everingham came a long run to Market Weighton, in which came Shipton Lane level crossing which was a block post open as required for any train wishing to use the single siding on the down side. This was at 1,486 yd. and was purely a road-side place where farmers could leave produce and collect items as required. Market Weighton was reached after 2 m. 8989 yd. with the line coming round eastwards over the York road to the West signal box or the north side of the level crossing.

Further back to the south west points had existed in single line days where the line became double at a cabin which handled the staff and token, this was Ballast Pit, a modest affair of 5 levers to the north of the line.

Everingham station, also muched improved latterly. C.T. Goode

MARKET WEIGHTON

Market Weighton is an old coaching village and originally a market at the point where five important highways met; the railways performed a similar service with four directions. The Roman road up from the Humber divided south of the town, one arm going east of it over the high Wolds to Malton, the west arm setting out for Stamford Bridge. Today the little town has reverted back more than a century to a quieter age, being freed from heavy road traffic by a southern by-pass. Mention should be made of William Bradley, an inhabitant of Market Weighton, who was 27 stone and almost eight feet tall. During his lifetime he was exhibited throughout the land and died in 1820. The prime buildings in the town were the church with a finely painted nave roof interior, and the station, both of which were well sited in the centre of things. The West signal box, where the Selby line met the York branch, was original and known first as Market Weighton Jc., with 18 levers and one spare. By the time the layout here had reached its final form, the number of levers had risen to 42, with eight spares, to do what had been previously accomplished with the smaller amount. One quirk was that the Selby arrival line was set back somewhat to join in behind the main-to-main crossover which now replaced it. At the other end of the station was the East Jc. where the Driffield and Beverley lines diverged. This, again was probably the original cabin, on the north side with 16 levers and a spare. When the Beverley line was doubled, sidings were put in on the town side with a slip to the Beverley line beyond the junction, while the number of levers, now all working, was increased to 18. East box controlled the yard outlet on the down side with its small engine shed of two roads, one of which went through to a turntable and warehouse built on to the side of it next to the station building. In the up yard were the goods shed, small petrol siding and coal drops adjacent to the gasworks.

Market Weighton station from the west.   D. Thompson

The station approach led to a longish, low building with a pillared portico at the passenger entrance. The platforms had an overall roof, as the other, more important local stations did, though when major repairs were needed, it was found easier to remove this and replace by ugly, tilted awnings on each side in 1947, a regrettable policy of the period.

Driffield's went the same way in 1949, along with that at Pickering. At the west end of the up platform was the wooden tea room, useful for passengers and staff alike which sported stained glass in its door and was owned by a lady called Tessa Uttley who moved, on closure, to Kiplingcotes station house. The station site is now cleared and is private housing; an attempt was made to preserve the frontage, but the portico was damaged by a reversing lorry.

Market Weighto from the forecourt. Note tearoom and tall chimneys. J.W. Armstrong

THE CLIMB TO ENTHORPE

A sharp contrast was presented to the through passenger between Selby and Driffield, for after Market Weighton the flat landscape gave way dramatically to rolling countryside with chalk cuttings and gradients through an area where the inhabitants live in scattered farms dotted at random. There was a long pull at 1 in 100 up to Enthorpe and, possibly for this reason the small engine shed was maintained at Market Weighton until 1918, from which to obtain assistance, if any train were to stick. However, local traffic seemed to manage, while heavy excursions were usually double-headed in any case, except for the odd, valiant little Midland 4F or LNER J11 0-6-0 which would come along and try its strength from time to time. Goodmanham village was close by the line, and Lord Hotham desired a station at this point; however, discussions brought his halt to Kiplingcotes on the York-Beverley line instead, though the site at Goodmanham was always kept in mind. A signal box was opened here, at 1,418 yd. to reduce the long block section at busy times. The cabin was in action at Grouping in 1923, but had vanished from the books by ten years later. Enthorpe station lay at the east end of the mile long cutting, at 2 m. 1,064 yd. from Goodmanham, the roadway attracting photographers at weekends during the summer months. There was nothing here to generate passengers, except a derelict chapel, the end of Kiplingcotes racecourse, used once a year, and the small Hall which gave the station its name. Kiplingcotes, named after a farm, was 2½ miles away. Dalton Hall and the Hotham family was 3 miles away at least. For all this the NER provided a decent sized, brick station building, one of the pleasantest anywhere with its Dutch roof, lost to admirers here, situated on the north platform with the station houses on the bank above it, while the small yard of two roads lay also on the north side. The facing platform had the signal box of 12 levers at the end of it with a good view down the cutting under the bridge. Probably as a retrenchment during the Great war, the line was singled from here to Southburn and was certainly still like this in 1922, though no reference has been unearthed as to what the working arrangements were. The line continued in several cuttings for 3 m. 302 yd., passing beneath the A 163 road and over a minor road to North Dalton to reach Middleton-on-the-Wolds where it then ran more to the east. The station building was a four square affair on the north platform, first of three similar ones, away from the village but in the goods yard of four roads with 5 ton crane and goods shed. The village was a large one, just south of the station and also on the main road. A small housing estate lay between the goods yard and the road nearby. The signal box was also on the north side of the line and had 16 levers, with 5 spare.

'Jubilee' No. 45646 'Napier' takes the Driffield line with its train. The spare enging in the siding adjacent could be either a casualty or a pilot   N. Stead

BAINTON AND SOUTHBURN

The line continued to fall until it reached level crossing country again, first at the gate box at Bainton Road on the A 163 road and then at Bainton station, at 1 m. 875 yd., one which was a last minute decision to construct, as was the level crossing which was installed instead of a bridge over the road. Bainton village was a good mile to the north of here, with its ancient church and close to Neswick Hall. At the station, both the main building, small yard with two ton crane and signal box of 17 levers were on the village side of things, with parallel platforms.

Enthorpe station, often hard to see, is clear here as D49 No. 62773 'The South Durham' pauses with a stopping train, though the headlamps show otherwise.
J.W. Armstrong

The buildings comprised a two storey section and a single storey portion with gable for each, linked by a transverse central section glassed in to the platform, a very neat and interesting assembly. The whole site with platforms is currently flourishing in private hands, though it does mean that bits are added on to the original outline as years come and go. There is also a small.surviving run of railwaymen's cottages across the road. Another tidy stretch, this time of 2 m. 1,093 yd. brought the railway to Southburn, where the village was situated conveniently to the west and where the surroundings were redolent of other 'burns'; Kirkburn, Eastburn and Battleburn High and Low. Now on the flat, the station took on a rather everyday appearance, with its main buildings on the north side, similar to those at Bainton but their mirror image. The yard, again with a small two ton crane ran off at a tangent to the roadway which came in over a skew level crossing, The signal box was on the south side by the gates, with its pointwork requiring a good heave at the levers, as it was a good distance away. When developments took place, a further siding was put in on the up side at the west end, running across to trail into the down line. There were 17 levers available to work the layout, of which one was spare. All has gone here, apart from the railway cottages.

Middleton-on-the-Wolds station. J.W. Armstrong

DOWN TO DRIFFIELD

We are almost at journey's end now though there is a run, still north east of 2 m. 884 yd. to Driffield West signal box and a further 506 yd., beyond to Driffield Jc., where the line joined the Hull-Bridlington route. There was only the gate box of Kelleythorpe with 8 levers, across the A 163 road shortly before Driffield West box across the A 163 road from Hull to Driffield was reached; both these crossings handled the same heavy road traffic to and from the seaside at weekends, and West box, on the south side of the line before 1900, then on the north side, saw off the single line to Malton. This began life, as single lines often did, as a double section which became one line after a short run round the corner. The branch was independent but became part of the NER in 1854, opening on 19th. May 1853. Its identity was preserved by someone's penchant for initialling; even the bricks were etched 'MDR'! Passenger trains ceased on 5th. June 1950 and complete closure came on 20th. October 1958 after a series of scenic excursions at various times, plus regular goods workings. The short section of line to Driffield Jc. was thus used to bring holidaymakers to and from the coast and gained an importance beyond its wildest dreams. Driffield West cabin had a 27 lever frame with 8 spares. From the Selby direction trains met with Outer and Inner distants and Outer and Inner Homes, while even the single line approach from Malton had two home signals, a true belt and braces situation.

Bainton station looking north. D. Thompson

Fitted in to the curve before Driffield Jc. was a siding on the north side trailing across into the up line and a similarly connected line to a turntable next to the signal box, presumably to cater for the Malton branch requirements and for the engines sent down from Bridlington for stabling off day excursions at times of pressure. This was done right into the 1960s and the author remembers 'Royal Scot' from Farnley Jc., spending a few relaxing hours here in the company of others out for the day. Once on the Hull-Bridlington line and past the cabin on the west side, followed by a cramped siding on each side with goods shed on the west,

Southburn station from the level crossing. D. Thompson

Driffield Station Gates cabin, a jolly wooden affair, again on the west side heralded Driffield station, with up and down platforms which were originally covered by an overall roof, gloomy but imposing. Right outside the station, which is close to the town itself was a three road goods yard and five ton crane; the exit ran alongside the down line for some way, picking up a three road coal depot and cattle dock across Wansford level crossing before ending in the running line at Meadow Gates signal box. From here in the up direction there was a turnout into a long line running parallel to the main line with, firstly, a run-round loop and an extra parallel line serving the Cake Mills of Messers.Barker, Sons & Co. just beyond Wansford crossing, then the goods depot and warehouse. This extra line was taken in just before the station was reached. A pilot shunting engine, often one of the 'Sentinels' was often to be seen at this point awaiting whatever work came along, though it no doubt drew the line at banking excursions up to Enthorpe!

Driffield was, and still remains, a small but vigorously independent town with a commercial life based originally on the roads and its canal which ran to a wharf just to the east of the station. There was a brisk traffic in all manner of goods by rail and a large cattle market not far from the railway near the Beck in the town.

Beyond Meadow Gates, a cabin which disappeared many years ago, the line runs on to Nafferton and Bridlington and is happily still in use.

'Black Five' No. 44932 enters Driffield round the curve from West Jc. The line off left is for Hull. *J. Taylor*

PASSENGER SERVICES

The first passenger service was three trains each way from York and two from Selby, and soon a suggestion was made that one engine might well be juggled to work both service, an idea with which the directors agreed, but which was not feasible. On Tuesdays, a market day, a train left Market Weighton at 6.30am to run to Selby,where Leeds passengers could change, and then reversing and on to Hull. A year later, the train started back at Pocklington and thus described a 'Z' shaped route on its travels. The increase in goods traffic at Market Weighton from 1851 caused the setting on of a clerk at 15/- a week. It must be remembered that in these early days both the York and Selby lines were single track, though the former must have been doubled by the opening of the single line to Beverley in 1865, as a new service of trains appeared, from York at 7.10am., 9.25, 3.30pm., and 7.00, and back from Hull at 6.45am., 9.40 and 2.45pm. There was also a fast 1.15pm. from Hull which took 1½ hours and stopping at Beverley, Market Weighton, Pocklington and Stamford Bridge. This connected with the 2.55 northbound express at York.

In 1866 there were four trains each way between Market Weighton and Selby, as follows:

		1	2	3	4
Market Weighton	dep: 8.35am	12.45pm	5.45	8.10
Harswell Gate	dep: 8.42		5.59	8.17
Holme Moor	dep: 8.47	1.10	5.59	8.22
Foggathorpe	dep: 8.56	1.20	6.09	8.31
Highfield	dep: 9.01	1.26	6.15	8.36
Bubwith	dep: 9.05	1.30	6.20	8.40
Menthorpe Gate	dep: 9.10		6.26	8.45
Duffield Gate	dep: 9.14		6.31	8.49
Cliff Common	dep: 9.18	1.53	6.35	8.53
Selby	arr: 9.25	2.00	6.45	9.00

1. Passenger and Cattle. 2. Passenger, Goods and Cattle. 3. Passenger and Cattle. 4. Passenger.

	1	2	3	4
Selby	dep: 7.15am	10.55	3.45pm	7.05
Cliff Common	dep: 7.22	11.03	3.55	7.12
Duffield Gate	dep: 7.26	11.06		7.16
Menthorpe Gate	dep: 7.30	11.11		7.20
Bubwith	dep: 7.35	11.17	4.15	7.25
High Field	dep 7.39	11 20	4 18	7 29
Foggathorpe	dep: 7.44	11.27	4.25	7.34
Holme Moor	dep: 7.53	11.37	4.35	7.43
Harswell Gate	dep: 7.58	11.45		7.48
Market Weighton	arr: 8.05	11.55	5.00	7.55

1. Passenger and Cattle. 2. Passenger and Goods. 3. Passenger and Cattle. 4. Passenger.

Driffield Jc. signal box   *C.T. Goode*

Market Weighton was still a terminus for some trains after the opening of the Hull line, and in 1885 there was still one Market Weighton to Hull mixed train at 1.30pm and one in the reverse direction at 1.46pm, probably Market Weighton shed turns. By 1908 Market Weighton's shed had one engine and crew, plus cleaner.

The only duty was the 7.54am to Driffield, 9.48 Driffield-Selby and 12.53pm Selby-Market Weighton. The shed closed on 1st. March 1917.

A meeting of B16s at Driffield. The left-hand one had failed.   *C.T. Goode*

As regards the Selby-Market Weighton line, there was a basic service of three trains each way throughout its life; certainly when the line was opened to Driffield things stayed much as they were, with the three running through.

June 1902.
Leeds	dep:	10.00	
Selby	dep: 8.40am	10.39	7.35pm
Market Weighton	dep: 9.23	11.05	8.25
Driffield	dep: 9.57	11.29	8.59
Bridlington	arr: 10.19	11.45	9.18
Bridlington	dep: 9.27am	7.15pm	8.00
Driffield	dep: 9.48	7.31	8.19
Market Weighton	dep: 10.23	8.07	8.43
Selby	dep: 11.05(arr)	8.50(arr)	9.10
Leeds	arr:		9.45

This could hardly be called a regular service throughout the day.

From the outset in 1889 the Driffield line had enjoyed a good service of trains, all of which ran to Bridlington as did the above, with several conditional stops. Enthorpe had at first visiting trains only on Weds., Thurs. and Sats., while before 1900 there were two morning expresses from Selby to Bridlington between ten and eleven each morning, while Enthorpe had five stoppers daily. Thereafter the service was moderated, as can be seen in the table opposite.

On the York-Hull line services improved, to eight each way in 1910, with two expresses of which the 5.05pm from Hull took 61 minutes.

Beneath the roof at Driffield. One of the staff is unusually tall.
Heyday Publishing Co.

During the Great War the service was reduced to five each way, retaining, however the expresses which took roughly the same overall time. Just prior to the outbreak of war in 1914, the Selby-Driffield line could show a fair amount of passenger train activity as shown below. Broadly speaking, there were five local trains to Selby and six down, plus one or two expresses and a morning Bridlington-Leeds run in 1¾ hours. Note also the morning runs each way between Bridlington and York. Footnotes limiting passengers' use of services at various stations were fashionable, while one wonders what induced the powers that be to start the afternoon slow from Market Weighton to Bridlington half an hour earlier on Thursdays only:

'Sentinel'shunter No. 68153 at Driffield, north end. *C.T. Goode*

Summer 1914.

Down

York	dep:6.35am	6.35								
Leeds	dep:	6.35	9.47	12.26pm	1.22	2.05				
Selby	dep:	8.37	10.18	1.18	2.05	2.33MO	3.40			
Cliff Com.	dep:	8.44	10.25	1.25		2.40	b			
Men. Gate	dep:	8.49		1.30		2.46				
Bubwith	dep:	8.53	10.32	1.34		2.51				
Highfield	dep:	8.56		1.37		2.54	b			
Fogga.	dep:	9.01	10.37	1.42		2.59				
Holme M.	dep:	9.08	10.43	1.49		3.06	b			
Evering.	dep:	9.12	10.48	1.54		3.11	b			
									ThO	ThX
Mkt. W.ton	dep:7.54x	9.19	10.54	2.01(arr)	2.28(arr)	3.18	4.10	2.07	2.33
Enthorpe	dep:8.04		11.06					sig	sig
Midd.-o-t-W	dep:8.10	9.34	11.12				4.26	2.23	2.49
Bainton	dep:8.14	9.38	11.16				sig	2.27	2.53
Southburn	dep:8.19		11.21				sig	2.32	2.58
Driffield	dep:8.25	9.47	11.26				4.11b	2.38	3.05
Bridlington	arr:9.12	10.12	11.44				4.59	2.56	3.23

b. sets down only.   x. arrives 28 minutes earlier.   sig. calls on request.
ThO. Thurs. only.   ThX. except Thurs.

York	dep:			
Leeds	dep:		4.57	6.35
Selby	dep:	4.55	5.37	7.30
Cliffe Common	dep:	5.02		7.37
Menthorpe Gate	dep:	5.07		7.42
Bubwith	dep:	5.11		7.46
Highfield	dep:	5.14		7.49
Foggathorpe	dep:	5.19		7.54
Holme Moor	dep:	5.26		8.01
Everingham	dep:	5.31		8.06
Market Weighton	dep:	5.38(arr)	6.00	8.13
Enthorpe	dep:		6.12	a
Middleton-o-t-w	dep:		6.18	8.38
Bainton	dep:		6.22	8.42
Southburn	dep:		6.27	a
Driffield	dep:		6.33b	8.54
Bridlington	arr:		6.53	9.14

a. Sets down from beyond Market Weighton. Takes up for beyond Driffield.

Down. Summer 1914

Bridlington dep:	6.30am	8.00		9.13	10.55	1.22pm	4.35	7.15
Driffield dep:	6.50	8.16		9.32	11.11	1.50	4.53	7.31
Southburn dep:	7.00			9.48	f	1.57	5.00	7.40
Bainton dep:	7.06			9.54	f	2.03	5.06	7.46
Midd.-o-t-w dep:	7.10		d	9.58	11.27	2.07	5.10	7.50
Enthorpe dep:	7.17			10.05		2.14	5.17	
Mkt. W.ton dep:	7.35x7.42	8.41		10.12	11.41	2.21	5.25	6.02	8.07
Everingam dep:		7.50	c	10.22	11.48	2.42	6.09 sig	
Holme Moor dep:		7.56		10.27	11.53	2.46	6.14 sig	
Foggath. dep:		8.03		10.33	11.59	2.52	6.20 sig	
Highfield dep:		8.08		10.37	12.03	2.56	6.24 sig	
Bubwith dep:		8.11		10.40	12.06	2.59	6.27	
Menth. Gt. dep:		8.16		10.44	12.10	3.03	6.31	
Cliffe Com. dep:		8.24		10.49	12.15	3.08	6.36	
Selby arr:		8.34	9.09	10.57	12.24	3.14	5.48	6.45	8.45
York arr:	8.32			(arr)				
Leeds arr:			9.45		2.23		6.26	7.52	10.13

d. stops for passengers for Leeds, York and beyond, also on Mondays. for Selby.   c. stops for passengers beyond Doncaster and Leeds.
f. takes up for York, Selby and beyond.   x. arrives 12 minutes earlier.

Small engine with long train. No. 43077 crosses Bainton Road crossing
M. Thompson

After 1923 the LNER improved the Hull-York service, with a return to seven trains each way. The 10.05 ex York took 61 minutes and 8.25 from Hull 60 minutes. The 12.40pm carried the palm by covering the distance to York in 56 minutes, stopping at Beverley only and connecting with the northbound 'Scotsman'. Possibly the most interesting was the Humber-Tyne restaurant car service which ran as follows:

Newcastle	dep: 12.10pm.	Hull	dep: 4.47pm
York(reversal)	dep: 2.18pm	Newcastle	arr: 8.19pm
Hull	arr: 3.17pm		

This was a round trip for locomotive and coaches; there were stops at Beverley, Market Weighton and Pocklington on the return leg.

Post war services on the Selby-Driffield line in 1922 were roughly on a par with what had gone before:

						SX*	
Selby	dep: 8.30am	1.18pm	2.17	4.05			5.50
Market Weighton	dep: 9.14	2.03	2.42	4.35			6.33
Driffield	dep: 9.49	2.35	3.07	5.02	6.11	7.05
Bridlington	arr: 10.14	2.51	3.21	5.18	6.27	7.21

*left Leeds at 4.52 and ran non-stop to Driffield.

Bridlington	dep: 7.20am	7.55		10.55	3.27pm	6.35
Driffield	dep: 7.39	8.13		11.15	3.45	6.53
Market Weighton	dep: 8.11	8.40		11.49	4.18	7 28x
Selby	arr: 8.54	**		12.27	4.57	8.05

** non-stop to Leeds, arrive 9.30
x.calls at Everingham, Foggathorpe, Highfield and Menthorpe Gate on request.

A fine shot of No. 61433 and its driver topping Enthorpe bank.   C. Ord

There was now a real effort to provide a fast service for commuters between Bridlington and Leeds, with one train taking only 1 hour 35 min. each way. The stretch between Enthorpe and Southburn was worked as a single line at this time. One small delight was a Mondays Only train which left Selby empty stock at 9.25am, arriving at Cliffe Common at 9.35am. to depart with passengers at 9.57am and reach Selby at 10.05am for the market day. Goods workings in 1922 were as follows:

Selby dep: 9.15am. Fast run to Market Weighton arr: 10.00.
Market Weighton dep: 10.30am and roadside stations to Driffield arr: 12.30pm. Driffield dep: 1.55pm and roadside stations to Market Weighton arr: 5.00pm. Thence a fast run back to Selby arr: 5.45pm.

A pick-up goods left Market Weighton at 1.30pm, arriving at Selby at 5.30.

The excursion business was in full swing right from the start, with summer seasonal holiday workings in 1868 operated by the L & YR on Wednesdays and Saturdays leaving Normanton at 3pm. to reach Scarborough at 6pm., the MR on Thursdays leaving Normanton at 2.45pm, arriving in Scarborough at 5.20pm and the NER's own on Wednesdays and Saturdays at 4.25pm from Leeds, reaching Scarborough at 8.05pm. An LNWR service also operated on the same days; this like all the other excursions, would run via York and Malton.

One of the rather strange Hughes 2-6-0s, No. 43760 desends Enthorpe bank towards Market Weighton. Note the tall home signal behind *C. Ord*

A day excursion was run on 28th. June 1895 from Southburn to Darlington, for the Agricultural Show, leaving at 6.30am and running via York to reach its venue at 9.30am. The return trip left at 5.15pm and arrived back in Southburn at 8.16pm.

By 1926 the Selby-Driffield service was roughly as in 1922, with all-stations trains from Selby at 8.30am. and 1.33pm., while the 5.50pm now wended its slow way right to Bridlington. The 2.17pm express now ran Saturdays only and the semi-fast at 4.05pm continued to run daily. The star turn, at 4.52pm from Leeds ran non-stop to Driffield as before, not Saturdays, but reached Bridlington five minutes earlier. In the up direction the stoppers to Selby left Bridlington at 7.17am, 10.55 and 3.27pm, with the semi fast at 6.35pm On Saturday there was a departure at 1.15pm from Bridlington non stop, reaching York at 2.12 via Market Weighton, a jolly good runner by any standards.

EXPERIMENTS IN LNER DAYS

'Sentinel' railcar No. 272 'Hero' in war time brown, makes its mark on the environment at Hull Paragon.   H.C. Casserley

At this period the LNER were making experiments with various types of rail cars, or motor buses as they were sometimes called in the timetables, and one of the latter was put into service on a working which left Selby at 4.42pm, reaching Market Weighton at 5.35, to return at 5.43 and arrive back in Selby at 6.38. The unit used would perhaps be one of the two NER petrol-electric railcars Nos. 3170/1 of 1903 which were stationed at Selby for a time in a lean-to shed of their own, or the petrol rail motor bus No. 130 which was a genuine adaptation of a road vehicle made in 1923 which again appeared at Selby after a trial-the shed staff must have been very tolerant in those days- and was known to have run out to Market Weighton and back as part of a busy schedule which took in far flung haunts such as Goole and Castleford in a single day. The table is well worth setting down:

	arr	dept
Selby		6.52am
Staddlethorpe	7.27	7.35
Goole	7.53	8.02
Selby	8.35	9.15
York	9.51	10.30
Selby	11.04	11.07
Goole	11.40	11.45
Selby	12.18pm	12.23
Castleford	12.58	1.17
Selby	1.53	3.24
Goole	3.57	4.02
Selby	4.33	4.42
Market Weighton	5.35	5.43
Selby	6.38	6.41
Cawood	6.58	7.02
Selby	7.19	7.22
Hemingbrough	7.28	7.39
Selby	7.44 (empty).	

The rail bus had a short life but a gay one, being destroyed in an accidental fire at Selby shed in 1926. At about this period the booking office at Selby was given a modern system of ticket issuing, known as the Passimeter, and tickets were issued in zones of fares charged; thus someone travelling, say, to Drax Hales on the Goole branch would find that his ticket was inscribed 'Wressle' which had the same fare, the idea saving the proliferation of ticket stock.

A B16 and 'Black Five' work in tandem to bring a holiday train up Enthorpe bank
C. Ord

From 1926 onwards there was a movement towards the use of the new 'Sentinel' and Clayton railcars powered by steam which would replace the ageing ex NER LNER G5 0-4-4s used on rural push-and-pull services in the Yorks. and Durham areas. The first railcar 'Valliant' (sic) came to Hull in May 1927, followed by a further twenty later on in that year; Selby acquired 'Waterwitch' and 'True Blue' in 1928, followed by 'Cleveland' at the end of that year. In 1929 'Surprise' came to Selby. By 1932 the number of cars at Selby had settled at two, while Bridlington had obtained one, 'Criterion' which claimed the record for the longest daily working of any such car, two return journeys of 42¾ miles to Selby and back in revenue earning service. 'Criterion' was the sole incumbent of its kind at Bridlington shed, from February 1931 to April 1941, when it went away to Neville Hill, Leeds. It was scrapped in November 1945.

The two round trips were, in 1932 the 11am and 3.25pm, the earlier one connecting at Selby with the Edinburgh-King's Cross train after the railcar had halted at each station on the way. The driver and fireman of the railcar (there were no guards on them) went on as passengers in the next train to Leeds and brought back the 4.53pm express to Bridlington, which now stopped at Market Weighton. This made use of the engine which had earlier reached Leeds on the 7.56 from Bridlington, whose crew next returned to Selby to pick up the railcar which now formed the 1.36pm Selby-Bridlington. The author hopes that the foregoing is clear; perhaps it is worth reading it again, for within it can be found the timetable of the line's train service for the period! As if the double run were not enough, 'Criterion' was turned out on returning home in 1933 on Weds. only for a late run to Hull, departing at 8.45pm all stations, returning from Hull at 10.50pm calling at principle stations and reaching Bridlington at 11.46pm-what might be termed as getting one's money's worth out of the rolling stock.

B16 No. 61419 breasts the summit at Enthorpe.   J.W. Armstrong

A steam locomotive, perhaps a D17 or D20 4-4-0 and four coaches (or a railcar loaned from Hull would appear in cases of debility or at busy times. By 1937 the double trips were always loco. hauled on Mondays and Sats.

The above notes were gleaned from the excellent survey 'Locomotives of the LNER' Vol.10B by the Railway Correspondence & Travel Society.

WARTIME AND LATTERLY

The hostilities of 1939-45 reduced the timetable to a basic three services each way, which called at all stations and, between Driffield and Bridlington, odd places conditionally, as Burton Agnes or Lowthorpe.

| Selby | dep: | 9.30am | 2.36pm | 5.48 |
| Bridlington | arr: | 11.03am | 4.09pm | 7.26 |

| Bridlington | dep: | 7.15am | 3.30pm | 6.58 |
| Selby | arr: | 8.52am | 5.00pm | 8.44 |

There was a 10.12am Mons. Only departure from Holme Moor which arrived at Selby at 10.39, a railcar working. There was, however, no great joy in commuting each day between Bridlington and Leeds. Off the 7.15am above, the arrival in Leeds was 9.45, while a return in Bridlington off the 5.10pm out of Leeds was at 7.26.

After the war the local services had to be dug out of a mass of summer Saturdays excursions which filled the columns of the timetable pages, making them seem to offer much more than they actually did. However, a search would find the following:

Selby   dep: 9.20am   2.30pm   6.08
Bridlington arr: 10.54am 3.58pm   7.40
The latter conveyed through carriages from Leeds, dep. 5.13pm.

Bridlington dep: 7.00am 3.45SX   4.00SO 7.00
Selby   arr: 8.36am 5.24pm   5.32   8.36

The latter ran on to Leeds, arr. 9.32 on Sats. Only.
Really this pattern was much the same as before; the Holme Moor departure on Mondays now left at 10.05am and reached Selby at 10.32. Additionally a daily train left Bridlington at 7.45am for York arr. 8.58, running via Driffield to call at Market Weighton at 8.20. There was also a similar SX departure from York at 7.55am, leaving Market Weighton at 8.55 and arriving at Bridlington at 9.35, shades of earlier days when similar trains ran. There were 17 booked summer Saturday workings to the coast and 18 in the reverse direction (See p.58).

The line from Market Weighton to York carried a goodly number of local passengers; not so that from Selby to Driffield which had been nurturing stations with hardly any customers for years. Thus, Menthorpe Gate only took £17 in 1940 in passenger fares, while Enthorpe and Everingham mustered up to £163 each.

Class D49 No. 62710 'Lincolnshire' awaits the arrival of the Bridlington coaches to take forward from Leeds   *C.T. Goode*

The big money spinners were Southburn earning £477 and Middleton-on-the Wolds at £1,615. The first closure came, however, on the York line with Holtby going to passengers on the outbreak of war in 1939 and to goods on 1st. January 1951, with Nunburnholme following suit completely in 1951. Menthorpe Gate began the belated closures on the Selby line, to passengers-there were some 40 or so potentials in the village-on 7th. December 1953. All other local stations were closed on 20th. September 1954. Enthorpe lost its goods yard on 14th. September 1959, with all the other intermediate stations losing theirs on 28th. January 1964 except Holme Moor and Everingham which kept theirs until 2nd. August 1965, the day on which the subject of this little book was relegated to history. For the record, Cherry Burton and Fangfoss closed to passengers on 5th. January 1959, while Kiplingcotes, which cannot have generated much passenger custom, stayed open but lost its goods yard after 1958. Passenger services on the York-Beverley-Market Weighton line were discontinued on 29th. November 1965 to considerable public outcry, chiefly over the loss of an alternative route from Hull.

Latterly the Selby-Bridlington service consisted of one working out of Selby at 9.20am, arriving Bridlington at 10.29 and one from Bridlington at 7.35am reaching Selby at 8.36 giving a connection for Leeds arriving there at 9.34am. The through coaches still left Leeds at 5.07pm SX, departing from Selby at 5.47 and reaching Bridlington at 6.58. One other train left Bridlington at 7.00pm to Market Weighton, with a connection for York at 7.50. By the last weeks of operation the latter service had been withdrawn. One had a feeling that the operating and shed staff at Bridlington had quite an enjoyable last fling in the days before the line was closed and the shed and its steam locomotives went the way of all good things. The 7.42am Hull-Bridlington dmu., was held at Driffield Jc. occasionally while the early Selby unit was put across in front of it; even better, there was one glorious morning when a whole bunch of horse boxes, apparently out of the yard at Burton Agnes, went round the corner to Selby behind an energetically steaming V3 tank engine. At one time in the 1960s the Craven dmus were withdrawn for adjustment and the old steamers of Bridlington shed came into their own for a time, enthusiastically pressed into action by their drivers, such as Arthur Dove, himself not far off retirement age.

Motive power on the line depended on either Selby or Bridlington sheds for the most part, the former having a good line in the hoarier NER goods 0-6-0s, small tanks and 4-4-0 varieties at various times, many of which looked decidedly seedy by the end of war in 1945. Bridlington had a small collection of D49 4-4-0s which were named after 'Hunts' and 'Shires' and which were well past their prime by the time retirement came along. The 5.07pm from Leeds would reach Selby, to be given its Bridlington D49 which had been panting, ready for action in the centre road (main line), perhaps relieving another D49 or B16 which would then press on towards Hull, lighter by a couple of coaches or so. The Brid. crew would set off with great panache over the swing bridge, first stop Market Weighton.

A B16 brings its train out of Selby to cross the bridge.   C.T. Goode

The railcars have been mentioned; these, named after stage coaches, were a bonny sight, firstly in red and cream, then green and cream livery until wartime placed some of them in a sort of institutional matt brown, though those which had retained the green and cream looked pretty dreadful after years of wartime neglect, plus living cheek by jowl with run-down steam engines. Often the rostered railcar would fail to appear and would be replaced by a G5 or a gasping D20 and couple of veteran coaches. Selby was at one time the hub of seven local services and the centre of a good system of zone tickets for local journeys. The engine shed was just south of the station and was memorable in that a spotter could easily gain entry and enjoy a fruitful look round before 'finding' the foreman whose office was on the far side. If he found you first, then much colourful language resulted!

THE DERWENT VALLEY LIGHT RAILWAY

As the independent Derwent Valley Light Railway impinged on the Selby to Market Weighton line at Cliffe Common, it is appropriate to mention it in some detail here. The idea stemmed from 1898,when, on 21st. March of that year the Riccall RDC proposed that a line be built, running from Barlby to Stamford Bridge, to bring the parishes involved 'into direct railway communication with the markets and towns'. Landowners were to be canvassed for their support. A Mr. Land, solicitor of Halifax, suggested one of those wilder schemes, that a line should run from Knottingley, then by Selby, through the areas of Riccall and Escrick to Bridlington and Scarborough, a suggestion which was soon dampened. On 29th. May 1899 there was a meeting between the Escrick and Flaxton RDCs and the NER to apply for a Light Railway Order for a line to run from Foss Islands, York, to Cliffe Common, to which the NER raised no objections. This Order was eventually confirmed by the Board of Trade as 'the Derwent Valley Light Railway Order of 1902 and it was found by enquiry that local landowners would be willing to contribute an annual total amount of £750 to the cause, not a great sum in fact. Four parish councils were against the order, along with 260 landowners and rate payers who would gain no benefit from the railway. The two original councils were deterred by the amount of finance likely to be involved, £100,000, and so the powers lapsed. A new Order, the DVLR Transfer Order, was applied for and granted in 1907, and a company was set up with a capital of £81,000 in £1 shares. The first directors included Lord Wenlock and Capt. Dunnington-Jefferson, together with one member of the NER Board, Mr. E.C.Geddes. The local councils still involved offered a dividend of 3% on Ordinary Share capital for ten years, to be repaid from a sinking fund in forty years after the opening of the line, which was duly done in 1953. Farmers were anxious to use the new railway which was now nearer for them than some of the NER premises which could be up to four miles away. This resulted in the section between Cliffe Common and Wheldrake opening as soon as it was completed, with the four stations thereon from 29th. October 1912 handling 9,568 tons of traffic over the seven miles of new track. The whole route was opened on 19th. July 1913 and totalled 20 miles 19 chains, of which just over four miles were sidings. The opening ceremony was performed by Lady Deramore, wife of the Chairman, at Layerthorpe, for which the first official train was of two coaches, two decorated wagons and brake van hauled by NER No. 1679 of Class X3. Engines and wagons were hired out from the NER, later LNER, and initially the two coaches were owned by the company, painted dark blue with gold lettering. The passenger service began on 21st. July 1913 (see p57).

In May 1908 a ten year working agreement was settled with the NER for through working of coal traffic and hiring of rolling stock, also a curbing of any likely competition locally, such as bus operation which might threaten DVLR passenger servies.

A fairly light train for once, hauled by No. 61468 at Bubwith.   *M. Thompson*

In the early days the DVLR provided a service on Mondays Only between Cliffe Common and Selby, for the market, and the brake van was lettered 'for use between Selby and Cliffe Common Only. Timetables are vague about this manoeuvre; there was a service from York at 9.40am which reached Cliffe Common at 10.30 and which would probably fill the bill, though the NER timetable gives no forward service to Selby. It is interesting to remember, however, that after 1923 a MO service to Selby from Cliffe Common did show up at about this time of day, probably as a substitute.

The greatest number of passengers carried was 49,983 in 1915; thereafter due to one thing or another a decline set in and by 1925 the returns showed 18,430 with a discontinuation of local passenger workings in 1926, though not before two Ford rail buses, used back-to-back had been purchased for use at the end of the NER agreement period. The bodies were by Chas. Roe of Leeds and each could seat 36. The affair was cheap to run, at 5p per mile and one wonders if it ever made contact with the similar sort of machine based at Selby shed and running round the district at this time. It was possible in theory on Saturdays only, when a service arrived at Cliffe Common from York at 4.40pm, before a service arrived from Selby, calling there at 4.52pm. Great imagination is called for here! In due course the two units were sold to the County Donegal Railways.

The route of the line was flat except for a gradient at the York end, and with plenty of level crossings. There were no signals, only one home made distant arm mounted on a post covering a more important crossing at Wheldrake. The station buildings were a pleasant bungalow type, of cricket pavilion appearance.

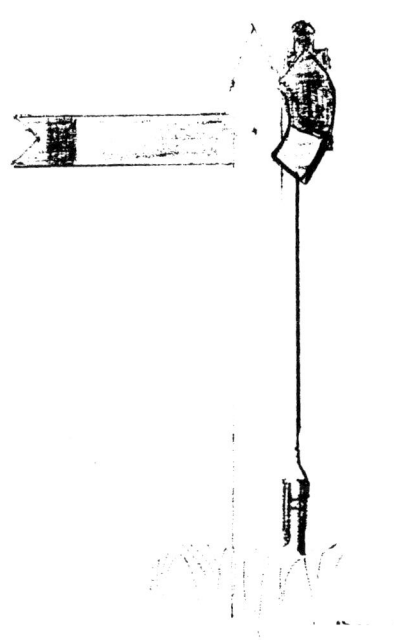

Weldrake

Excursions did take place, as in August 1928 when three left for Skipwith at 9.30am., 1pm. and 7pm., returning at 1045am., 5.45pm and 8pm. In the same month an excursion went to Bridlington via Cliffe Common. Eighty farmers went to the Royal Show at Harrogate in 1929 and were transferred across to the main station at York by bus. The Skipwith excursions were most likely blackberry ones, run to pick the fruit; travellers would be greeted on arrival by station staff who would indicate where the choicest pickings were to be found. Very evocative, this, of happier times when every day was a sunny one and the rails shimmered in the heat.

In 1932 an excursion conveyed 386 passengers to Scarborough. However, it was left to the groups of railway enthusiasts to field the largest tours; on 20th. June 1954, a Sunday, the RCTS chartered a six coach train from Sheffield Midland to tour the interesting parts of South Yorkshire, after which it took the 250 on from Cliffe Common to York, while in May 1958 the Branch Line Society went from Layerthorpe to Cliffe Common and return, using a three coach special hauled by J 21 No. 65064 which was borrowed from Darlington to replace the diesel shunter usually provided by British Rail for working the line at this time.

The excursion par excellence was part of a joint RCTS / Stephenson Locomotive Society special which took in the line to Cliffe Common on 27th. November 1963, the train comprising five coaches with dining car, headed by BR engine No. 46409. It is interesting to know that a line which was 'light' could stand up to this sort of heavy traffic without giving way at the seams, through wartime had brought with it all kinds of military use from installations set up en route. The trackbed was allowed to become weed overgrown to bamboozle the enemy, a likely story!

Closure of the BR line nearby meant that the DVLR had now become a dead-end from the north, with the result that the section from Wheldrake to Cliffe Common, which had opened first of all, was abandoned as from 9th. February 1965, with successive closures of the rest to Dunnington, where the small industrial estate survived for a time into the eighties, serviced from Layerthorpe and with the running of a steam passenger train or two using the preserved J72 'Joem', until the inevitable total closure. The line was indeed fortunate to survive as long as it did in its independent fashion.

APPENDICES

August 1950

								Suns.
Leeds	dep:			9.25		5.07		10.25am
Selby	dep:	9.20am		10.08	2.20pm	5.45	6.20	
		SO	SX			SX		
York	dep:	7.50	9.50			5.13		
Mkt Wn.	dep:	10.02	9.05	10.35	3.02 5.55	6.12	7.02	
Driffield	dep:	10.34	9.30	11.00	3.33 6.16	6.37	7.33	
Bridlington	arr:	10.54	9.45 11.01	11.18*3.49	6.32	6.58	7.49	12.09pmx

* 1 to Filey Holiday Camp   SO arr. 11.47.   x 3rd. Class only.

Bridlington	dep:	7.00am	7.45	3.45pma	4.40SX	7.00	6.50SX	7.50	8.40pm
Driffield	dep:	7.25	8.00	4.03	5.06	7.17		8.06	
Mkt. Wn.	dep:	7.26	8.20	4.35	5.26(arr)	7.53		8.30	
York	arr:		8.58				8.01		
Selby	arr:	8.36		5.15arr.		8.36		8.55(dep)	
Leeds	arr:							10.23	10.23x

a 15 mins. later throughout SO.   x 3rd. Class only.

Holme Moor dep. 10.05am MO,   arr Selby 10.32.

December 1951.

Leeds	dep:				5.07	
Selby	dep:		9.20		5.45	6.20
York	dep:	7.53am	5.15pmSX			
Mkt. Wn.	dep:	8.55	10.02	5.55	6.17	7.02
Driffield	dep:	9.19	10.34	6.19	6.37	7.35
Bridlington	arr:	9.35	10.54	6.35**	6.58	7.51

** calls at Middleton-on-the-Wolds at 6.07.   No Sunday trains.

Bridlington	dep:	7.00am	7.45		4.40pm	7.00
Driffield	dep:	7.25	8.00		5.06	7.17
Mkt. Wn.	dep:	7.56	8.20		5.26+	7.58
York	arr:		8.58		6.25	
Selby	arr:	8.36				8.41
Leeds		No through service.		No Sunday trains.		

+ Change

Traffic passing Lowthorpe Station (between Driffield and Bridlington). Saturday, 9th. August 1952. All are excursions unless stated otherwise. Towards Bridlington. Signal box open at 6.15am. Signalman R. Edmond.

6.17 in section. Hull-Scarborough.

6.25 Bridlington goods.

6.40 Hull-Bridlington. (calls)

8.14 Five light engines.

8.22 Hull-Scarborough. (calls)

8.41 Bradford-Filey Camp.

9.17 Hull Scarborough.

9.25 Leeds Bridlington.

9.36 Hull-Scarborough.

9.43 Market Weighton-Bridlington.

9.47 Sheffield-Bridlington.

9.54 Light engine.

10.03 Excursion not logged.

10.10 Excursion from Rotherham.

10.44 Excursion from Selby.

10.51 Excursion from Leeds.

10.57 Hull-Scarborough.

11.02 Excursion, defaced tab.

11.05 Leeds-Filey Camp.

11.30 Hull-Scarborough. (calls)

11.40 Excursion from Hazel Grove.

12.04pm York-Filey Camp.

12.09 Hull Bridlington.

12.16 Excursion from Bradford.

12.20 Excursion from Chesterfield.

12.28 Excursion from Blackburn.

12.37 Excursion from Stalybridge.

12.44 Excursion from Leicester.

12.59 Manchester-Filey Camp.

1.12 Hull-Bridlington.

1.17 Excursion from Sowerby Bridge.

1.20 Excursion from Silkstone.

1.33 King's Cross-Filey Camp.

1.39 Sheffield Vic.-Filey Camp.

1.50 Hull-Scarborough.

1.59 Worcester-Filey Camp.

2.10 Excursion from Basford.

2.17 Liverpool-Scarborough.

2.25 York-Filey Camp.

2.34 Excursion From Manchester.

2.49 Hull-Scarborough (calls).

2.56 Excursion from Holmfirth.

3.12 Hull-Scarborough.

3.56 Selby-Bridlington.

4.21 Hull-Scarborough.

4.42 York-Filey Camp.

5.20 Hull-Bridlington. (calls)

6.39 Hull-Scarborough. (calls)

7.31 Hull-Bridlington.

7.38 Selby-Bridlington.

Afternoon signalman J.Helm.

Towards Hull and Selby.

6.20am in section Light engine ('Sentinel')
6.38 Bridlington-Hull.
7.11 Bridlington-Selby.
7.25 Bridlington-Hull. (calls)
7.51 Bridlington-Market Weighton.
8.10 Bridlington-Hull.
8.35 Scarborough-Hull. (calls)
9.05 Scarborough-Hull.
9.25 Scarborough-Hull. (calls)
9.35 Filey Camp-Newcastle.
9.50 Return exc. to Kidsgrove.
10.05 Return exc. to King's Norton.
10.20 Return exc. to York.
10.37 Return exc. to Sheffield.
10.44 Return exc. to Kidsgrove.
10.52 Return exc. to Whetstone.
11.03 Bridlington-Hull.
11.19 Return exc. to York.
11.22 Filey Camp-King's Cross.
11.35 Return exc. to Leeds.
11.43 Return exc. to Manchester.
11.55 Return exc. not logged.
12.07pm Return exc. to Sheffield.
12.12 Light engine.
12.22 Scarborough-Hull.
12.27 Return exc. to Leeds.
12.44 Return exc. to Liverpool.
12.55 Scarborou-Hull. (calls)
1.06 Return exc. to Londesborough.
1.35 Return exc. not Logged.

1.43 Return exc. to Rotherham.
1.55 Return exc. to Sowerby Bridge.
2.08 Return exc. Derby. (unclear)
2.14 Return exc. to Sheffield.
2.35 Scarborough-Hull. (calls)
2.43 Return exc. to Bradford.
2.59 Return exc. to Leicester.
3.05 Bridlington-Hull.
3.14 Empty coaching stock.
3.22 Light engine.
3.18 Return exc. to Basford.
3.50 Bridlington-Hull. (calls)
3.58 Bridlington-Selby.
4.06 Light engine.
4.13 Light engine.
4.36 empty coaching stock.
4.49 empty coaching stock.
5.01 Bridlington-Hull. (calls)
5.27 Bridlington-Hull goods.
5.39 Bridlington-Hull. (calls)
6.46 Bridlington-Hull. (Calls)
7.02 Scarborough-Hull.
7.12 Bridlington-Selby.
7.31 Scarborough-Hull.
7.42 Empty coaching stock.
8.04 Bidlington York.
8.08 Empty coaching stock.
8.15 Scarborough-Hull goods.

Box closed 8.20pm

Passenger and excursion services. Sunday, 10th. August. 1952. Passing Lowthorpe towards Scarborough.

11.09am	in block. Hull-Scarborough.
11.10	from Castleford.
11.13	from Kippax.
11.51	from Leeds.
12.01pm	from Leeds.
12.06	from Rotherham.
12.15	from Selby.
12.26	from Wadsley Bridge.
12.32	from Hull.
12.40	from Marsden.
12.46	from Bradford.
12.53	from Mexborough.
1.21.	from Clayton.

Return excursions towards Hull and Selby.

7.07pm	to Selby; in block.
7.08	to Hull.
7.18	to Hull.
7.31	to Mexborough.
7.42	to Castleford.
7.53	to Wadsley Bridge.
8.01	to Hull.
8.11	to Marsden.
8.21	to Rotherham.
8.33	to Kippax.
8.42	to Mexborough.
9.00	to Hull.
9.13	to Bradford.
9.27	to Leeds.
9.34	to Hull.
9.46	to Clayton.
9.53	Staff Special.

DERWENT VALLEY LIGHT RAILWAY PROVISIONAL TIMETABLE:
JULY—30th SEPTEMBER, 1913.
Subject to alteration, of which due notice will be given.

WEEKDAYS—UP

		a.m.	p.m.	p.m.	p.m.	p.m.
York (Layerthorpe)	dep.	9.50	2.8	4.45	6.33	7.5
Osbaldwick		9.55	2.13	4.50	6.38	7.10
Murton Lane		9.58	2.16	4.53	6.41	7.13
Dunnington Halt		10.2	2.20	4.57	6.45	7.17
Dunnington (for Kexby)		10.6	2.24	5.1	6.49	7.21
Elvington (for Sutton)		10.12	2.30	5.7	6.55	7.27
Wheldrake		10.18	2.36	5.13	7.1	7.33
Cottingwith		10.22	2.40	5.17	S.E.	S.O.
Thorganby		10.26	2.44	5.21		
Skipwith & N. Duffield		10.31	2.49	5.26		
Cliff Common (D.V.L.)	arr.	10.38	2.56	5.33		
Cliff Common (N.E.)	dep.	10.49	3.8			
Selby (N.E.)	arr.	10.57	3.14			

WEEKDAYS—DOWN

		a.m.	a.m.	a.m.	p.m.	p.m.	p.m.
Selby (N.E.)	dep.				3.40	4.38	
Cliff Common (N.E.)	arr.				3.47	4.45	
Cliff Common (N.E.—from Market Weighton line)	arr.		10.49				
						S.E.	S.O.
Cliff Common (D.V.L.) dep.	8.0		11.0	3.50	5.40	6.10	
Skipwith & N. Duffield	8.7		11.7	3.57	5.47	6.17	
Thorganby	8.12		11.12	4.2	5.52	6.22	
Cottingwith	8.16		11.17	4.6	5.56	6.26	
Wheldrake	8.20	8.25	11.21	4.10	6.0	6.30	
Elvington (for Sutton)	TH & SO	8.31	11.27	4.16	6.6	6.36	
Dunnington (for Kexby)		8.37	11.33	4.22	6.12	6.42	
Dunnington Halt		8.41	11.37	4.26	6.16	6.46	
Murton Lane		8.46	11.42	4.31	6.21	6.51	
Osbaldwick		8.49	11.46	4.34	6.24	6.54	
York (Layerthorpe) arr.		8.53	11.50	4.38	6.28	6.58	

57

Table 25

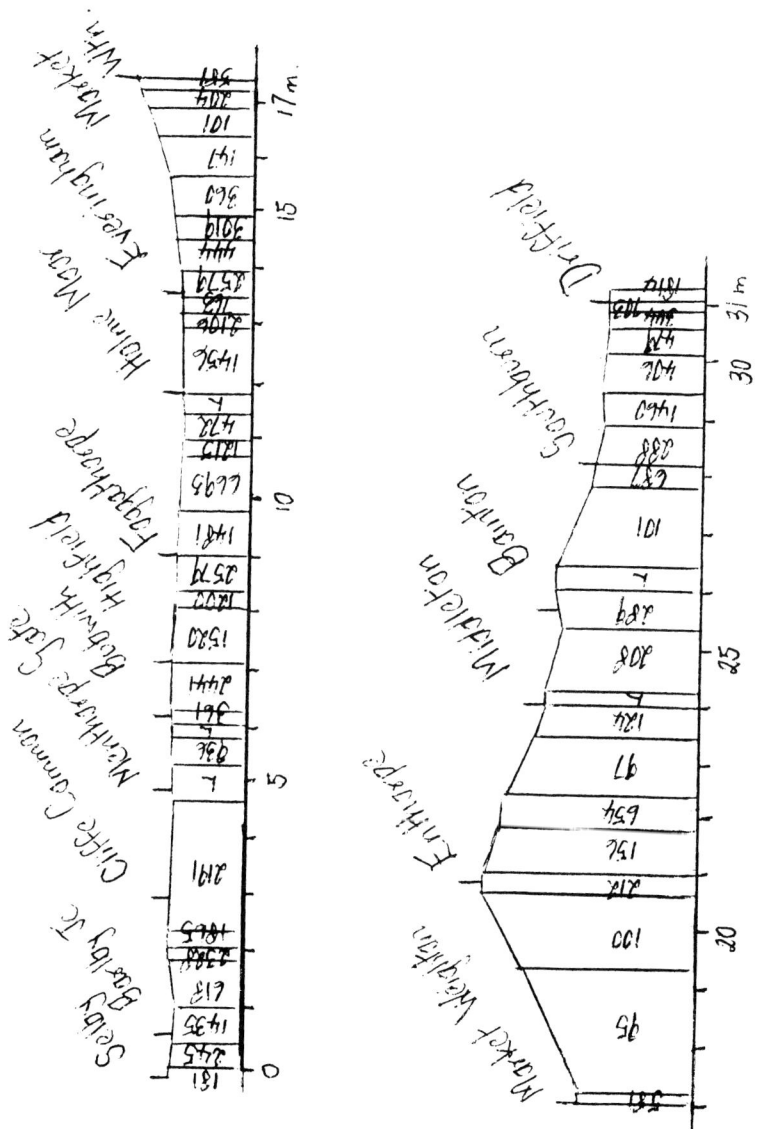

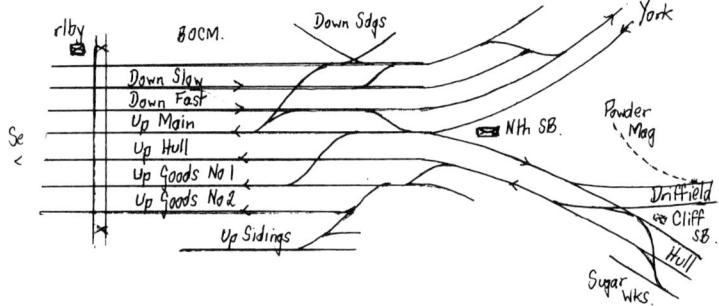

Barlby Junction

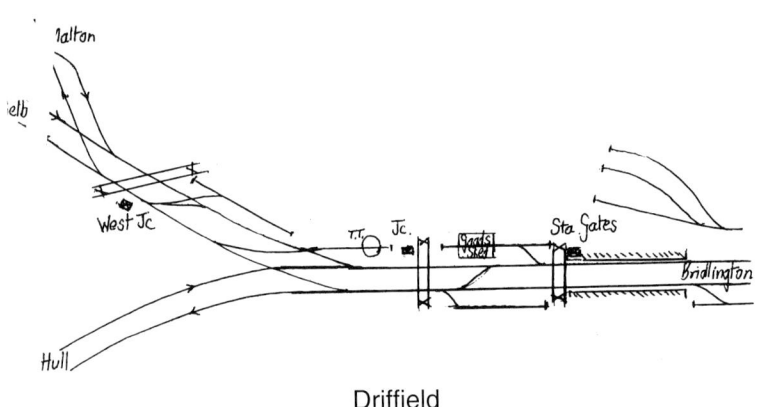

Driffield

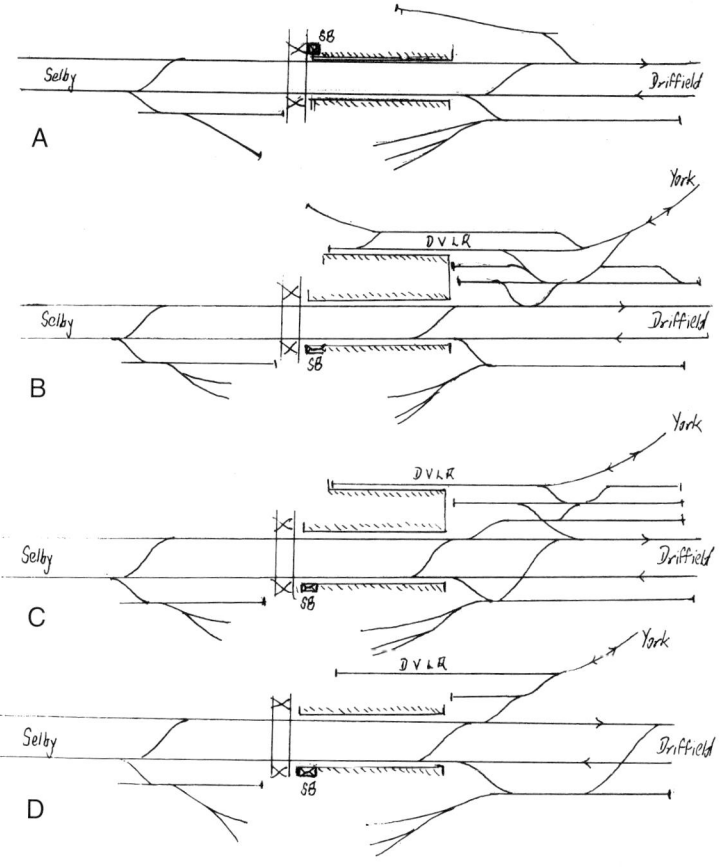

Developments at Cliffe Common

A 1902 B 1913 C 1948 D 1960
C Offers no direct access to the DVLR.

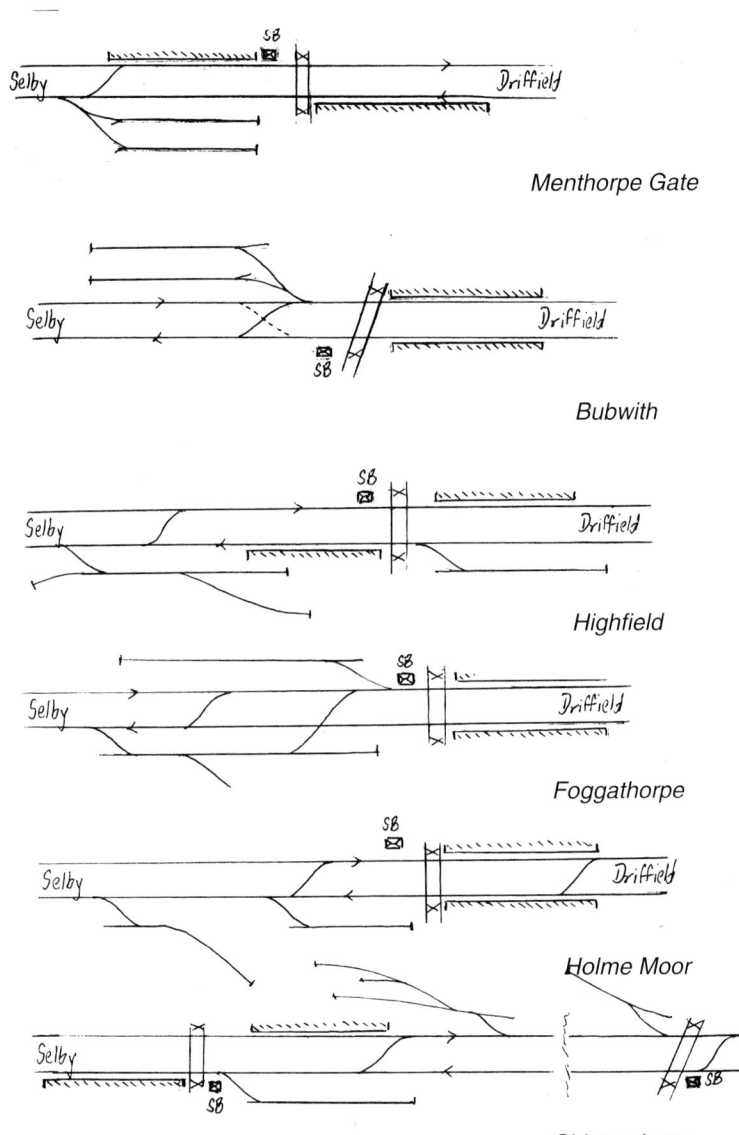

Menthorpe Gate

Bubwith

Highfield

Foggathorpe

Holme Moor

Everingham

Shipton Lane

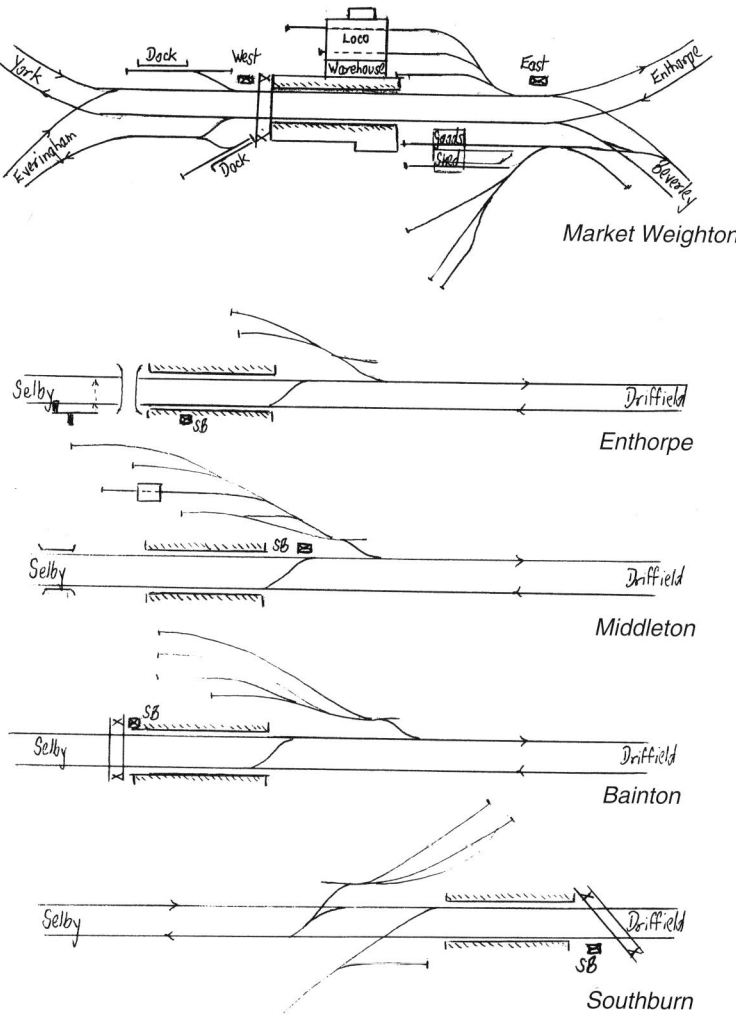

Market Weighton

Enthorpe

Middleton

Bainton

Southburn

Other books by the same Author:

'The Railways of Hull.'
'The Railways of Nottingham.'
'The Railways of Castleford.'
'Railways in South Yorkshire '
'The Railways of North Lincolnshire.'
'Huddersfield Branch Lines.'
'The Ashbourne-Buxton Railway.'
'The GN & GE Joint Railway.'
'The Trentham Gardens Branch.'
'The Dearne Valley Railway.'
'The Railways of Strathmore.'
'The Wakefield & Goole Railway' (late 1993).